DEFENSES

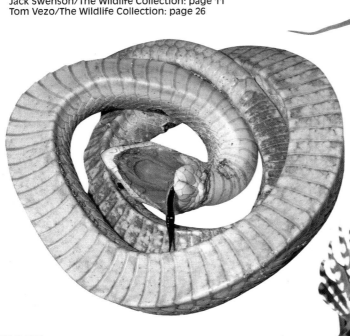

DEFENSES

WRITTEN BY

REBECCA L. GRAMBO

kidsbooks
Incorporated

For most animals, life is full of danger. One of the biggest threats is an attack from another animal. To avoid becoming someone's prey, animals use defenses.

The starfish will sacrifice one of its arms to an attacker. It does this to gain time to escape. Eventually, the starfish will grow a new arm to take the place of the one it gave away.

Armadillos rely on armor. They are covered with tough, flexible plates. When they are scared, armadillos curl into a ball to protect their head and stomach. Their built-in armor keeps them safe.

Prickly protection—that's what the hedgehog has. Its sharp spines are actually special hairs. The hedge-hog rolls into a tight ball to cover its unprotected areas. When it does this, the skin stretches and makes the spines stick out.

Many animals run away from danger. This kangaroo's strong hind legs will carry it quickly away from trouble.

SAFETY IN NUMBERS

Traveling in a group can be a lifesaver for animals.

Some kinds of birds live in large groups. They often do this when they are raising their young. With so many others around, a bird has less chance of being the one that a predator eats.

Many kinds of fish live in groups called schools. Schools of fish move together almost like they are one big animal. The movements of the school can be confusing to predators.

When muskoxen (MUSK-ox-un) are threatened by predators like wolves, they form a circle. The calves stand in the center. The adults face outward to keep an eye on the danger. The muskoxen lower their heads so they can use their horns to defend themselves.

Animals that eat plants often live together in groups. A herd of zebras is safer than one zebra by itself. There are more eyes to watch for danger.

BEAT IT!

One way to escape danger is to run—or swim—away. A frightened octopus first shoots out a dark cloud of ink. At the same time the octopus turns very pale. A predator may concentrate on the dark blob of ink in front of it. Meanwhile, the octopus can slip away.

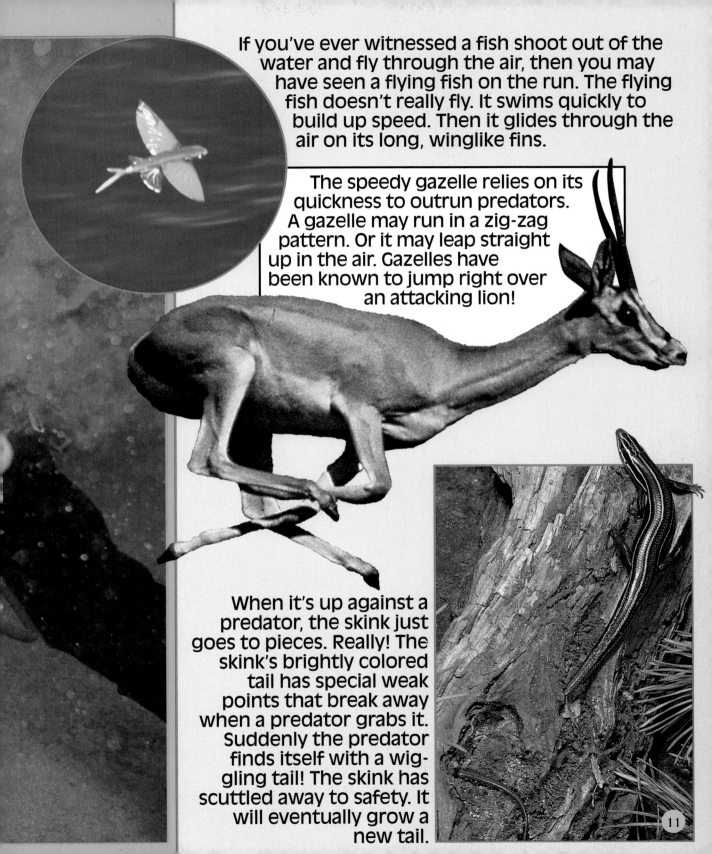

If you've ever witnessed a fish shoot out of the water and fly through the air, then you may have seen a flying fish on the run. The flying fish doesn't really fly. It swims quickly to build up speed. Then it glides through the air on its long, winglike fins.

The speedy gazelle relies on its quickness to outrun predators. A gazelle may run in a zig-zag pattern. Or it may leap straight up in the air. Gazelles have been known to jump right over an attacking lion!

When it's up against a predator, the skink just goes to pieces. Really! The skink's brightly colored tail has special weak points that break away when a predator grabs it. Suddenly the predator finds itself with a wiggling tail! The skink has scuttled away to safety. It will eventually grow a new tail.

SIZE SURPRISE!

Changing appearance is one way to escape an attack. It can scare or confuse a predator. Some animals can even make themselves *seem* too big to eat.

The pufferfish doesn't look intimidating when it's swimming around. But when it's scared, the pufferfish transforms into a round ball that's hard to swallow. It does this by filling itself with water.

To frighten its enemies, the frilled lizard acts big and tough. It opens its mouth wide, and spreads the flaps of skin on its neck. Then, standing up on its hind legs, the lizard runs!

Many toads react to danger by taking big gulps of air. This makes the toad swell up and look bigger. Some toads stand on their tiptoes to be even more scary looking.

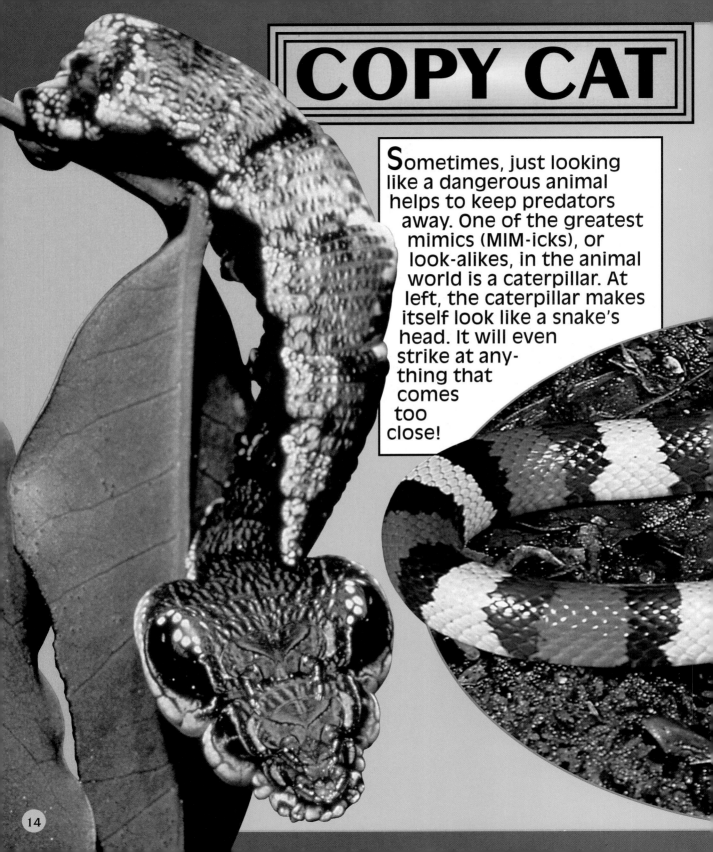

COPY CAT

Sometimes, just looking like a dangerous animal helps to keep predators away. One of the greatest mimics (MIM-icks), or look-alikes, in the animal world is a caterpillar. At left, the caterpillar makes itself look like a snake's head. It will even strike at anything that comes too close!

The scarlet king snake isn't poisonous, but it looks like a snake that is—the coral snake. Each snake has the same colors. The difference is the order in which the colors appear. Red separated by yellow bands means it's a poisonous coral snake. On the harmless king snake, red is separated by black bands.

Hover flies don't carry a stinger in their tail, but they fly and behave like bees. They even eat the same foods.

I SMELL

Many animals make bad smells to keep predators away. Some of them have a foul goo that oozes out of their body. Other animals deliver the stink directly to the enemy!

Almost everyone knows not to get too close to a skunk! When frightened, a skunk often gives a warning by stamping its front feet or doing a handstand. After that—look out! A skunk sprays a very smelly fluid from glands near its tail. It can spray up to 10 feet.

Stink bugs like this one can leave a "stink trail" where they've been feeding. Many of these smelly insects are brightly colored. This warns predators that attacking could really raise a stink!

Any animal deciding to snack on a bombardier (bom-buh-DEER) beetle is in for an unhappy surprise. When the beetle is attacked, chemicals inside its body mix together and make a hot, stinky liquid. With a very accurate aim, the beetle points its rear end at its attacker and sprays.

SUITS OF ARMOR

Our skeletons are inside our bodies. A crab's skeleton is the shell on the outside of its soft body. The tough, flexible shell protects the crab. As the crab gets bigger, it outgrows, or sheds, its shell. Until its new, bigger shell hardens, the crab is not protected.

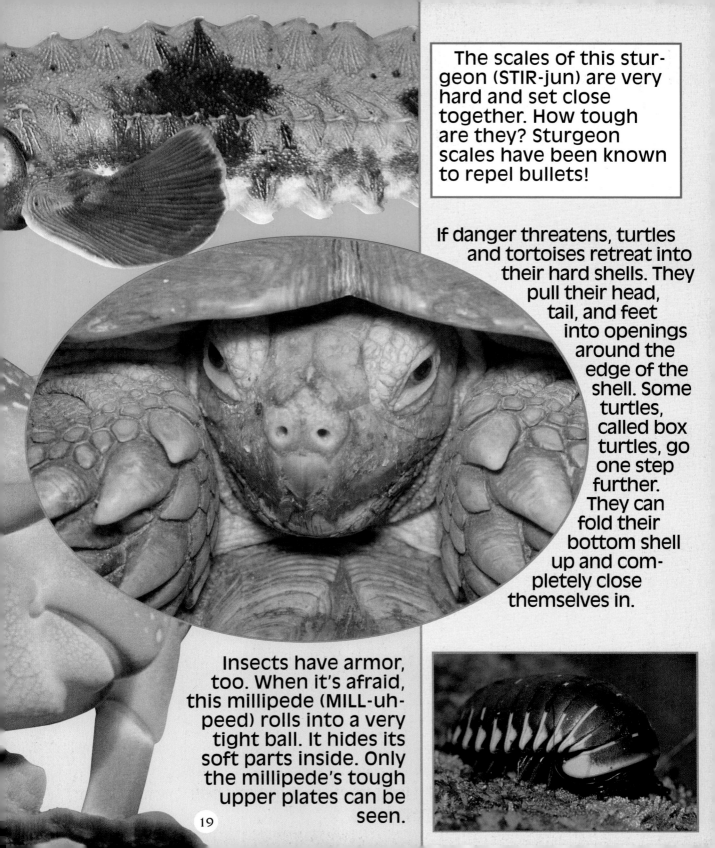

The scales of this sturgeon (STIR-jun) are very hard and set close together. How tough are they? Sturgeon scales have been known to repel bullets!

If danger threatens, turtles and tortoises retreat into their hard shells. They pull their head, tail, and feet into openings around the edge of the shell. Some turtles, called box turtles, go one step further. They can fold their bottom shell up and completely close themselves in.

Insects have armor, too. When it's afraid, this millipede (MILL-uh-peed) rolls into a very tight ball. It hides its soft parts inside. Only the millipede's tough upper plates can be seen.

PLAYING DEAD

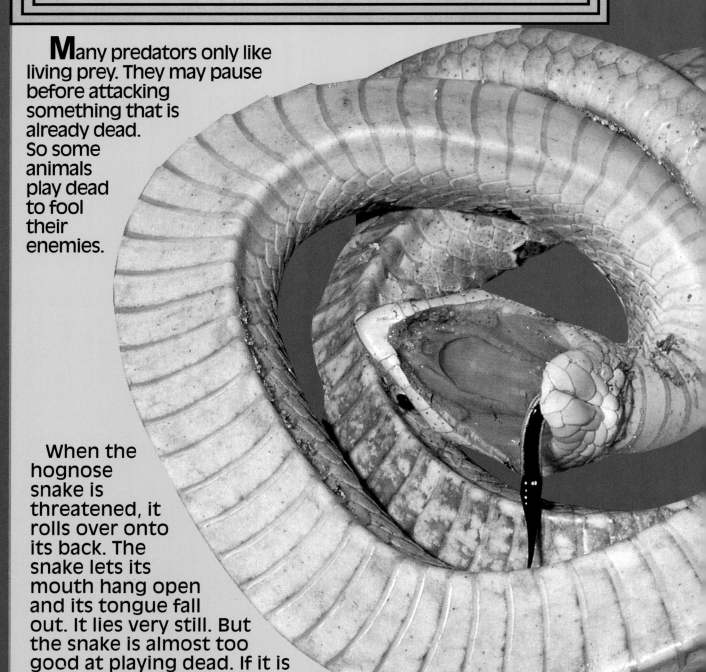

Many predators only like living prey. They may pause before attacking something that is already dead. So some animals play dead to fool their enemies.

When the hognose snake is threatened, it rolls over onto its back. The snake lets its mouth hang open and its tongue fall out. It lies very still. But the snake is almost too good at playing dead. If it is turned right side up, the snake flips itself back over!

20

If an opossum (A-pas-em) is attacked, it will fight back. If that doesn't work, the opossum "drops dead." It lies on the ground without moving, even if it is bitten by its attacker. When danger has passed, the opossum slowly gets up and scurries off.

The killdeer doesn't play dead to protect itself. But to protect its nest from a predator, the killdeer puts on an act. It pretends to be hurt and calls loudly to get the animal's attention. When it has lured the predator far enough away from the nest, the killdeer suddenly runs or flies away.

DON'T TOUCH ME

The long spines of a sea urchin are poisonous. Not many animals will try to eat a sea urchin.

Some animals use spines or stingers for protection.

When threatened, the porcupine raises its sharp quills (kwills). It keeps its quill-filled rear end pointed at the attacker. Porcupines can't throw their quills. But the quills come out of the porcupine's skin very easily. Just brushing against a porcu-pine can be painful.

The lionfish is beautiful but deadly. Inside its frilly fins are sharp poisonous spines. Lionfish are very easy to spot. But predators leave them alone.

The clownfish doesn't have spines, quills, or poison. But it lives with someone who does—the anemone (uh-NEM-oh-nees). Anemones look like plants but are really animals. The clownfish is protected from predators by hiding in the anemone's stinging tentacles. The sting doesn't hurt the clownfish, though. The clownfish has a layer of slime on its body that protects it from the anemone.

YOU CAN'T SEE ME

You can't eat what you can't find. That's why many animals use camouflage (CAM-o-flahj) to hide. By blending into the background, they make it hard for predators to see them.

Deer fawns hide from danger by standing or lying very still. The white dots on their coat look like the spotty light coming through the trees or grass. In this field, a fawn's spots blend in very well with the clover blossoms around it.

These white ptarmigan (TAR-mi-gun) are hard to see in the snow. Only their black eyes and beaks show. When they tuck their heads under their wings, they seem to disappear. In the summer, ptarmigan turn brown to blend in with the ground and trees.

This dead leaf has eyes! Actually, the "leaf" is a butterfly's wing. By resembling the dead leaves around it, the butterfly can hide from predators. Its wings even have spots that look like bugs have been feeding on them.

You might look right at this caterpillar and never know it was there. Some caterpillars hide by looking just like part of a plant. It would take a very sharp-eyed bird to spot this one!

YUCK!

Lovely to look at, yucky to eat! Some animals are poisonous or just taste bad. A predator who has never seen one of these animals may try to eat it. But after the first time—no way! The bright colors of these bad-tasting animals warn off the predator.

The monarch (MON-ark) butterfly is bright orange and black. Those colors warn hungry birds to leave the monarch alone. Birds know that monarchs taste bad.

Usually, this toad keeps its green side up. But when it's scared, it lives up to its name—fire-bellied toad. The toad flips onto its back and shows off its bright red-and-black underside. Predators know to leave this poisonous toad alone.

Predators who try to eat the nudibranch (NUDE-uh-brank) get two surprises. Not only does the nudibranch taste bad, but it can sting, too.

This caterpillar doesn't just taste icky. Those sharp, pointy bristles will give an attacker a bad rash. Birds and other predators avoid caterpillars that look like this.

FIGHTING BACK

When some animals are threatened, they don't run away. They fight back! Claws, teeth, antlers, and tusks can all be used as weapons.

Very few people would want to argue with either of these animals. Both the Cape buffalo and the warthog are very good at defending themselves. Cape buffaloes may weigh a ton, and they seem to have bad tempers. They will charge at almost anything that moves, including lions! Warthogs often run from danger. But when they are cornered, they will fight back with their sharp tusks.

Rattlesnakes would rather run away than fight. But if they have to fight, they are well armed. Their poisonous fangs can deliver a dangerous bite. Rattlesnakes get their name from the noise they make by vibrating the end of their tail. Sometimes they make this noise as a warning before they strike, but not always.

In every group of termites, there are soldiers—termites with big, strong jaws. These termites are in charge of guarding the rest of the group from enemies like ants. The soldiers protect the entrances to their home. They also protect other termites who are out gathering food.